Angels Address Book

ANGELS ADDRESS BOOK

A directory of angels and friends

PEONY PRESS

This edition is published by Peony Press, an imprint of Anness Publishing Ltd, Hermes House,
88–89 Blackfriars Road, London SE1 8HA; tel. 020 7401 2077; fax 020 7633 9499
www.peonypress.com; www.annesspublishing.com

Publisher: Joanna Lorenz
Editorial Manager: Joanne Rippin
Designer: Andrew Heath

A CIP catalogue record for this book is available from the British Library

IMPORTANT ADDRESSES

A

B

> Oh, hush the noise,
> ye men of strife,
> And hear the angels sing!
>
> *It Came upon the Midnight Clear*

C

D

E

F

G

H

I

J

K

L

M

N

O

P

Q

R

S

T

U

V

W

X

Y

Z

A

Name

Address

Telephone

Name

Address

Telephone

Name

Address

Telephone

Name

Address

Telephone

Name

Address

Telephone

Name

Address

Telephone

Name

Address

Telephone

Name

Address

Telephone

Four angels to my bed,
Four angels round my head,
One to watch, and one to pray,
And two to bear my soul away.

THOMAS ADY
A Candle in the Dark

Name

Address

Telephone

Name

Address

Telephone

Name

Address

Telephone

A

Name
Address

Telephone

Name
Address

Telephone

Name
Address

Telephone

Name
Address

Telephone

Name
Address

Telephone

Name
Address

Telephone

For he shall give his angels
charge over thee,
to keep thee in all
thy ways.

Psalm 91, v. 11

Name
Address

Telephone

Name
Address

Telephone

Name
Address

Telephone

Name
Address

Telephone

WHY was Cupid a boy?
And why a boy was he?
He should have been a girl,
For aught that I can see.

For he shoots with his bow,
And the girl shoots with her eye;
And they both are merry and glad,
And laugh when we do cry.

Then to make Cupid a boy
Was surely a woman's plan,
For a boy never learns so much
Till he has become a man.

And then he's so pierced with cares,
And wounded with arrowy smarts,
That the whole business of his life
Is to pick out the heads of the darts.

WILLIAM BLAKE *Cupid*

B

Name
Address

Telephone

Name
Address

Telephone

Name
Address

Telephone

Name
Address

Telephone

Name
Address

Telephone

Name
Address

Telephone

Name
Address

Telephone

Name
Address

Telephone

Name
Address

Telephone

The angels all were singing
out of tune,
And hoarse with having little
else to do,
Excepting to wind up the sun
and moon,
Or curb a runaway young
star or two.

GEORGE GORDON,
LORD BYRON
The Vision of Judgement

Name
Address

Telephone

B

Name

Address

Telephone

Name

Address

Telephone

Name

Address

Telephone

Name

Address

Telephone

Name

Address

Telephone

Name

Address

Telephone

Name

Address

Telephone

Name

Address

Telephone

Twice or thrice had
I loved thee
Before I knew thy face or name,
So in a voice, so in a
shapeless flame,
Angels affect us oft, and
worshipped be.

JOHN DONNE
Air and Angels

Name

Address

Telephone

Name

Address

Telephone

PLACE the helm on thy brow,
  In thy hand take the spear;
Thou art arm'd, Cupid, now,
  And thy battle-hour is near.
March on! march on! thy shaft and bow
  Were weak against such charms;
March on! march on! so proud a foe
  Scorns all but martial arms.

See the darts in her eyes,
  Tipt with scorn, how they shine!
Ev'ry shaft, as it flies,
  Mocking proudly at thine.
March on! march on! thy feather'd darts
  Soft bosoms soon might move;
But ruder arms to ruder hearts
  Must teach what 'tis to love.
Place the helm on thy brow;
  In thy hand take the spear, –
Thou art arm'd, Cupid, now,
  And thy battle-hour is near.

THOMAS MOORE *Cupid Armed*

C

Name ....
Address ....
....
....
Telephone ....

Once at the Angelus
(Ere I was dead),
Angels all glorious
Came to my bed;
Angels in blue and white,
Crowned on the head.

AUSTIN DOBSON
Good Night, Babette

Name ....
Address ....
....
....
Telephone ....

Name ....
Address ....
....
....
Telephone ....

Name ....
Address ....
....
....
Telephone ....

Name ....
Address ....
....
....
Telephone ....

Name ....
Address ....
....
....
Telephone ....

Name ....
Address ....
....
....
Telephone ....

Name ....
Address ....
....
....
Telephone ....

Name ....
Address ....
....
....
Telephone ....

Name ....
Address ....
....
....
Telephone ....

Name ....
Address ....
....
....
Telephone ....

Name ....
Address ....
....
....
Telephone ....

C

But in his motion like
an angel sings.
Still quiring to the young-eyed
cherubims.

WILLIAM SHAKESPEARE
The Merchant of Venice

Name
Address

Telephone

Name
Address

Telephone

Name
Address

Telephone

Name
Address

Telephone

Name
Address

Telephone

Name
Address

Telephone

Name
Address

Telephone

Name
Address

Telephone

Name
Address

Telephone

Name
Address

Telephone

Name
Address

Telephone

Name
Address

Telephone

AND feeble, exhausted, unawares she took
To gazing on the god, – till, look by look,
   Her eyes with larger life did fill and glow.
She saw his golden head alight with curls, –
   She might have guessed their brightness in the dark
   By that ambrosial smell of heavenly mark!
She saw the milky brow, more pure than pearls,
   The purple of the cheeks, divinely sundered
By the globed ringlets, as they glided free,
Some back, some forwards, – all so radiantly . . .

ELIZABETH BARRETT BROWNING *Psyche Gazing on Cupid*

D

Name

Address

Telephone

Name

Address

Telephone

Name

Address

Telephone

Name

Address

Telephone

Name

Address

Telephone

Name

Address

Telephone

Name

Address

Telephone

It is not because angels are
holier than
men or devils that makes
them angels,
but because they do not
expect holiness
from one another, but from
God only.

WILLIAM BLAKE

A Vision of the Last Judgement

Name

Address

Telephone

Name

Address

Telephone

D

Name ....
Address ....
....
....
Telephone ....

Name ....
Address ....
....
....
Telephone ....

Name ....
Address ....
....
....
Telephone ....

Name ....
Address ....
....
....
Telephone ....

Name ....
Address ....
....
....
Telephone ....

Name ....
Address ....
....
....
Telephone ....

Name ....
Address ....
....
....
Telephone ....

Name ....
Address ....
....
....
Telephone ....

Name ....
Address ....
....
....
Telephone ....

Name ....
Address ....
....
....
Telephone ....

Not where the wheeling
systems darken,
And our benumbed
conceiving soars!
The drift of pinions,
we would harken,
Beats at our own
clay-shuttered doors.
The angels keep their
ancient places;
Turn but a stone,
and start a wing!

FRANCIS THOMPSON
The Kingdom of God

Eros, from rest in isles far-famed,
With rising Anthesterion rose,
And all Hellenic heights acclaimed
  Eros.

The sea one pearl, the shore one rose,
All round him all the flower-month flamed
And lightened, laughing off repose.

Earth's heart, sublime and unashamed,
Knew, even perchance as man's heart knows,
The thirst of all men's nature named
  Eros.

ALGERNON CHARLES SWINBURNE *Eros*

E

Name ....
Address ....
....
....
Telephone ....

Name ....
Address ....
....
....
Telephone ....

Name ....
Address ....
....
....
Telephone ....

Name ....
Address ....
....
....
Telephone ....

Name ....
Address ....
....
....
Telephone ....

Name ....
Address ....
....
....
Telephone ....

Name ....
Address ....
....
....
Telephone ....

Name ....
Address ....
....
....
Telephone ....

The angels are so enamoured of the language that is spoken in heaven, that they will not distort their lips with the hissing and unmusical dialects of men...

RALPH WALDO EMERSON

Essays

Name ....
Address ....
....
....
Telephone ....

Name ....
Address ....
....
....
Telephone ....

E

Name

Address

Telephone

Name

Address

Telephone

Name

Address

Telephone

Name

Address

Telephone

Name

Address

Telephone

Name

Address

Telephone

There are nine orders of angels, to wit, angels, archangels, virtues, powers, principalities, dominations, thrones, cherubim and seraphim.

POPE GREGORY THE GREAT
Homilies

Name

Address

Telephone

Name

Address

Telephone

Name

Address

Telephone

Name

Address

Telephone

I looked over Jordan, and what did I see,
Comin' for to carry me home?
A band of angels comin' after me,
Comin' for to carry me home.

ANON

F

Name
Address

Telephone

Name
Address

Telephone

Name
Address

Telephone

Name
Address

Telephone

Name
Address

Telephone

Name
Address

Telephone

Name
Address

Telephone

Let brotherly love continue.
Be not forgetful to entertain strangers, for thereby some have entertained angels unawares.

St Paul's Epistle to the Hebrews, Chapter 13, vv. 1–2

Name
Address

Telephone

Name
Address

Telephone

Name
Address

Telephone

F

Name
Address

Telephone

Name
Address

Telephone

Name
Address

Telephone

Name
Address

Telephone

Name
Address

Telephone

Name
Address

Telephone

It is not known precisely
where angels dwell –
whether in the air, the void
or the planets.
It has not been God's pleasure
that we should
be informed of their abode.

VOLTAIRE
Philosophical Dictionary

Name
Address

Telephone

Name
Address

Telephone

Name
Address

Telephone

Name
Address

Telephone

Music the fiercest grief can charm,
And fate's severest rage disarm;
Music can soften pain to ease,
And make despair and madness please:
Our joys below it can improve,
And antedate the bliss above.
This the divine Cecilia found,
And to her Maker's praise confined the sound.
When the full organ joins the tuneful quire,
The immortal powers incline their ear;
Borne on the swelling notes our souls aspire,
While solemn airs improve the sacred fire;
And angels lean from heaven to hear.
Of Orpheus now no more let poets tell,
To bright Cecilia greater power is given;
His numbers raised a shade from hell,
Hers lift the soul to heaven.

ALEXANDER POPE *Ode on St Cecilia's Day*

G

Name
Address

Telephone

Name
Address

Telephone

Name
Address

Telephone

Praise be to Allah,
the creator of the
heavens and earth,
who makest the
angels his messengers,
and giveth them two, three
or four pairs of wings.

The Koran, XXXV

Name
Address

Telephone

Name
Address

Telephone

Name
Address

Telephone

Name
Address

Telephone

Name
Address

Telephone

Name
Address

Telephone

Name
Address

Telephone

Name
Address

Telephone

G

Name
Address

Telephone

Name
Address

Telephone

Name
Address

Telephone

Name
Address

Telephone

Name
Address

Telephone

Name
Address

Telephone

The angels are the dispensers and administrators of the Divine beneficence towards us; they regard our safety, undertake our defence, direct our ways, and exercise a constant solicitude that no evil befalls us.

JOHN CALVIN
Institutes of the Christian Religion

Name
Address

Telephone

Name
Address

Telephone

Name
Address

Telephone

Name
Address

Telephone

H

Name
Address

Telephone

I have always found that angels have the vanity to speak of themselves as the only wise; this they do with a confident insolence sprouting from systematic reasoning.

WILLIAM BLAKE
The Marriage of Heaven and Hell

Name
Address

Telephone

Name
Address

Telephone

Name
Address

Telephone

Name
Address

Telephone

Name
Address

Telephone

Name
Address

Telephone

Name
Address

Telephone

Name
Address

Telephone

Name
Address

Telephone

Name
Address

Telephone

J

Name ....
Address ....
....
....
Telephone ....

Name ....
Address ....
....
....
Telephone ....

Name ....
Address ....
....
....
Telephone ....

I want to be an angel,
And with the angels stand,
A crown upon my forehead,
A harp within my hand.

URANIA BAILEY
I Want to be an Angel

Name ....
Address ....
....
....
Telephone ....

Name ....
Address ....
....
....
Telephone ....

Name ....
Address ....
....
....
Telephone ....

Name ....
Address ....
....
....
Telephone ....

Name ....
Address ....
....
....
Telephone ....

Name ....
Address ....
....
....
Telephone ....

Name ....
Address ....
....
....
Telephone ....

J

Name ....
Address ....
....
....
Telephone ....

Name ....
Address ....
....
....
Telephone ....

Name ....
Address ....
....
....
Telephone ....

Name ....
Address ....
....
....
Telephone ....

Name ....
Address ....
....
....
Telephone ....

Name ....
Address ....
....
....
Telephone ....

Name ....
Address ....
....
....
Telephone ....

Name ....
Address ....
....
....
Telephone ....

Name ....
Address ....
....
....
Telephone ....

We not only live among men, but there are airy hosts, blessed spectators, sympathetic lookers-on, that see and know and appreciate our thoughts and feelings and acts.

H.W. BEECHER
Royal Truths

Name ....
Address ....
....
....
Telephone ....

Name ....
Address ....
....
....
Telephone ....

K

Name ....
Address ....
....
....
Telephone ....

Name ....
Address ....
....
....
Telephone ....

Name ....
Address ....
....
....
Telephone ....

Name ....
Address ....
....
....
Telephone ....

Name ....
Address ....
....
....
Telephone ....

Name ....
Address ....
....
....
Telephone ....

Name ....
Address ....
....
....
Telephone ....

Name ....
Address ....
....
....
Telephone ....

Name ....
Address ....
....
....
Telephone ....

At the round earth's
imagined corners, blow
Your trumpets, Angels,
and arise, arise
From death,
you numberless infinities
Of souls.

JOHN DONNE
Holy Sonnets VII

Name ....
Address ....
....
....
Telephone ....

IN Heaven a spirit doth dwell
'Whose heart-strings are a lute';
None sing so wildly well
As the angel Israfel,
And the giddy stars (so legends tell),
Ceasing their hymns, attend the spell
Of his voice, all mute.

And they say (the starry choir
And the other listening things)
That Israfeli's fire
Is owing to that lyre
By which he sits and sings –
The trembling living wire
Of those unusual strings.

If I could dwell
Where Israfel
Hath dwelt, and he where I,
He might not sing so wildly well
A mortal melody,
While a bolder note than this might swell
From my lyre within the sky.

EDGAR ALLAN POE *Israfel*

ADORAMVS TE GLORIFICAM
ADORAMVS TE GLORIF
MVS E GLO

L

Name ....
Address ....
....
....
Telephone ....

Name ....
Address ....
....
....
Telephone ....

Aerial spirits,
by great Jove designed
To be on earth the
guardians of mankind.

HESIOD
Works and Days

Name ....
Address ....
....
....
Telephone ....

Name ....
Address ....
....
....
Telephone ....

Name ....
Address ....
....
....
Telephone ....

Name ....
Address ....
....
....
Telephone ....

Name ....
Address ....
....
....
Telephone ....

Name ....
Address ....
....
....
Telephone ....

Name ....
Address ....
....
....
Telephone ....

Name ....
Address ....
....
....
Telephone ....

Name ....
Address ....
....
....
Telephone ....

M

Name
Address

Telephone

Name
Address

Telephone

Name
Address

Telephone

Name
Address

Telephone

Name
Address

Telephone

On the second day,
God created the angels,
with their natural propensity
to good.

Midrash

Name
Address

Telephone

Name
Address

Telephone

Name
Address

Telephone

Name
Address

Telephone

Name
Address

Telephone

No sooner had th' Almighty ceased, but all
The multitude of angels with a shout,
Loud as from numbers without number, sweet
As from blest voices, uttering joy, heav'n rung
With jubilee, and loud hosannas filled
The eternal regions . . .

Then, crowned again, their golden harps they took,
Harps ever tuned, that glittering by their side
Like quivers hung, and with preamble sweet
Of charming symphony they introduce
Their sacred song, and waken raptures high;
No voice exempt, no voice but well could join
Melodious part, such concord is in heaven.

JOHN MILTON *Paradise Lost*

N

Name
Address

Telephone

Name
Address

Telephone

Name
Address

Telephone

Name
Address

Telephone

Name
Address

Telephone

Name
Address

Telephone

Name
Address

Telephone

Name
Address

Telephone

> Salvation may be earned
> through an angel,
> but a livelihood requires the
> intervention of God.
>
> SAMUEL B. NAHMAN

Name
Address

Telephone

Name
Address

Telephone

Name
Address

Telephone

O

Name

Address

Telephone

Name

Address

Telephone

Name

Address

Telephone

Name

Address

Telephone

Name

Address

Telephone

Name

Address

Telephone

The language in which God, angels and men spoke together, not through the ambiguous murmur of a Castillian spring, Typhonian cave or Dorian wood, but as friends talk face to face.

REUCHLIN

De Merifico Verbo

Name

Address

Telephone

Name

Address

Telephone

Name

Address

Telephone

Name

Address

Telephone

ANGEL spirits of sleep,
White-robed, with silver hair,
In your meadows fair,
Where the willows weep,
And the sad moonbeam
On the gliding stream
Writes her scattered dream:

Angel spirits of sleep,
Dancing to the weir
In the hollow roar
Of its waters deep;
Know ye how men say
That ye haunt no more
Isle and grassy shore
With your moonlit play;
That ye dance not here;
White-robed spirits of sleep,
All the summer night
Threading dances light?

ROBERT BRIDGES *Spirits*

P

Name

Address

Telephone

Name

Address

Telephone

Name

Address

Telephone

Name

Address

Telephone

Name

Address

Telephone

Name

Address

Telephone

Name

Address

Telephone

Name

Address

Telephone

Name

Address

Telephone

Name

Address

Telephone

The angel Gabriel from
heaven came
With wings as white as snow
and eyes like flame.
'All hail,' said he, 'Thou
blessed virgin Mary,
Most high favoured lady.'
Gloria.

SABINE BARING-GOULD

Q

Name
Address

Telephone

Name
Address

Telephone

Name
Address

Telephone

Name
Address

Telephone

Name
Address

Telephone

Name
Address

Telephone

The angels all did sing
Praises to our heavenly King,
And peace to man living,
With right good will.

Melismata

Name
Address

Telephone

Name
Address

Telephone

Name
Address

Telephone

Name
Address

Telephone

Name
Address

Telephone

MORE than a thousand jubilant Angels saw I,
Each differing in effulgence and in kind.

DANTE *Paradiso*

R

Name
Address

Telephone

Name
Address

Telephone

Name
Address

Telephone

Name
Address

Telephone

Name
Address

Telephone

Name
Address

Telephone

Name
Address

Telephone

Name
Address

Telephone

Name
Address

Telephone

And I saw another sign in heaven, great and marvellous, seven angels having the seven last plagues; for in them is filled up the wrath of God.

The Book of Revelation, Chapter 15, v. 1

Name
Address

Telephone

Name
Address

Telephone

S

And the angel said unto me, Wherefore didst thou marvel?

The Book of Revelation, Chapter 17, v. 7

Name

Address

Telephone

Name

Address

Telephone

Name

Address

Telephone

Name

Address

Telephone

Name

Address

Telephone

Name

Address

Telephone

Name

Address

Telephone

Name

Address

Telephone

Name

Address

Telephone

Name

Address

Telephone

AND at that centre, with their wings expanded,
More than a thousand jubilant Angels saw I,
Each differing in effulgence and in kind.
I saw there at their sports and at their songs
A beauty smiling, which the gladness was
Within the eyes of all the other saints;
And if I had in speaking as much wealth
As in imagining, I should not dare
To attempt the smallest part of its delight.

DANTE *Paradiso*

HARK! the herald Angels sing
Glory to the new-born King.
Peace on earth, and mercy mild,
God and sinners reconciled.
Joyful all ye nations, rise,
Join the triumph of the skies;
With the Angelic host proclaim,
Christ is born in Bethlehem.
  Hark! the herald Angels sing
  Glory to the new-born King.

CHARLES WESLEY
Hark, the Herald Angels Sing

T

Name
Address

Telephone

Name
Address

Telephone

Name
Address

Telephone

And I saw an angel come down from heaven, having the key of the bottomless pit and a great chain in his hand.

The Book of Revelation, Chapter 20, v. 1

Name
Address

Telephone

Name
Address

Telephone

Name
Address

Telephone

Name
Address

Telephone

Name
Address

Telephone

Name
Address

Telephone

Name
Address

Telephone

Name
Address

Telephone

U

Name ....
Address ....
....
....
Telephone ....

Name ....
Address ....
....
....
Telephone ....

Name ....
Address ....
....
....
Telephone ....

Name ....
Address ....
....
....
Telephone ....

Name ....
Address ....
....
....
Telephone ....

Name ....
Address ....
....
....
Telephone ....

And he dreamed,
and behold a ladder set up
on the earth,
and the top of it reached
to heaven:
and behold the angels of
God ascending and
descending on it.

The Book of Genesis,
Chapter 28, v. 12

Name ....
Address ....
....
....
Telephone ....

Name ....
Address ....
....
....
Telephone ....

Name ....
Address ....
....
....
Telephone ....

MINE Eye doth pierce the heavens, and see
What is Invisible to thee.
My garments are not silk nor gold,
Nor such like trash which Earth doth hold,
But Royal Robes I shall have on,
More glorious than the glistring Sun;
My Crown not Diamonds, Pearls, and Gold,
But such as Angels heads infold.
The City where I hope to dwell,
There's none on Earth can Parallel:
The stately Walls both high and strong,
Are made of pretious Jasper stone;
The Gates of Pearl, both rich and clear,
And Angels are for Porters there;
The Streets thereof transparent gold,
Such as no Eye did e're behold;
A Chrystal River there doth run,
Which doth proceed from the Lamb's Throne.

ANNE BRADSTREET *The Flesh and the Spirit*

V

Name ....
Address ....
....
....
Telephone ....

Name ....
Address ....
....
....
Telephone ....

Name ....
Address ....
....
....
Telephone ....

Name ....
Address ....
....
....
Telephone ....

Name ....
Address ....
....
....
Telephone ....

The helmed Cherubim
And sworded Seraphim
Are seen in glittering ranks
with wings display'd,
Harping in loud and
solemn quire.

J. MILTON
Ode on the Morning of Christ's Nativity

Name ....
Address ....
....
....
Telephone ....

Name ....
Address ....
....
....
Telephone ....

Name ....
Address ....
....
....
Telephone ....

Name ....
Address ....
....
....
Telephone ....

Name ....
Address ....
....
....
Telephone ....

W

Name ....
Address ....
....
....
Telephone ....

Name ....
Address ....
....
....
Telephone ....

Name ....
Address ....
....
....
Telephone ....

Name ....
Address ....
....
....
Telephone ....

Name ....
Address ....
....
....
Telephone ....
....

Name ....
Address ....
....
....
Telephone ....

Name ....
Address ....
....
....
Telephone ....

But if they rush dreadful,
The angels, most heedful,
Receive each mild spirit,
New worlds to inherit.

WILLIAM BLAKE
Night

Name ....
Address ....
....
....
Telephone ....

Name ....
Address ....
....
....
Telephone ....

Name ....
Address ....
....
....
Telephone ....

LET them praise Thy Name, let them praise Thee, the supercelestial people, Thine angels, who have no need to gaze up at this firmament, or by reading to know of Thy word. For they always behold Thy face, and there read without any syllables in time, what willeth Thy eternal will; they read, they choose, they love. They are ever reading; and that never passes away which they read; for by choosing, and by loving, they read the very unchangeableness of Thy counsel. Their book is never closed, nor their scroll folded up; seeing Thou Thyself art this to them, and art eternally; because Thou hast ordained them above this firmament, which Thou hast firmly settled over the infirmity of the lower people, where they might gaze up and learn Thy mercy, announcing in time Thee Who madest times. For Thy mercy, O Lord, is in the heavens, and Thy truth reacheth unto the clouds. The clouds pass away, but the heaven abideth.

SAINT AUGUSTINE *Confessions*

X

Name
Address
Telephone

While mortals sleep,
the angels keep
Their watch of
wondering love.

O Little Town of Bethlehem

Name
Address
Telephone

Name
Address
Telephone

Name
Address
Telephone

Name
Address
Telephone

Name
Address
Telephone

Name
Address
Telephone

Name
Address
Telephone

Name
Address
Telephone

Name
Address
Telephone

Name
Address
Telephone

Y Z

Name
Address

Telephone

Name
Address

Telephone

Name
Address

Telephone

Name
Address

Telephone

Name
Address

Telephone

Ding dong! verily the sky
is riven with
angels singing.

Ding dong!
Merrily on High

Name
Address

Telephone

Name
Address

Telephone

Name
Address

Telephone

Name
Address

Telephone

Name
Address

Telephone

Name
Address

Telephone

ACKNOWLEDGEMENTS

The following pictures are reproduced with kind permission of the Bridgeman Art Library, London:

Front jacket: *Annunciation* by Filippino Lippi (c1457/8–1504) Galleria dell'Accademia, Florence. p2 Detail of angels from the altarpiece at St Barnabas by Sandro Botticelli (144/5–1510) Galleria degli Uffizi, Florence. p8 *Cupid and Psyche* by Annie Swynnerton (1844–1933) Oldham Art Gallery, Lancs. p9 *Cupidon*, 1891 by William-Adolphe Bouguereau (1825–1905), Roy miles Gallery, 29 Bruton Street, London W1. p13 *Cupid Carving a Bow* by Francesco (Mazzola) Parmigianino (1503–40) Kunsthistorisches Museum, Vienna/Ali Meyer. p16 *Cupid: on Guard* by Thomas Stothard (1755–1834) Simon Carter Gallery, Woodbridge. p16/17 *Cupid and Psyche* by Paolo di Matties (1662–1728) Christie's, London. p20/21 Votive offering of Louis X1V by Nicolas Mignard (1606–68° Chateau de Versailles, France/Giraudon. p24 *Four Angels Playing Instruments* by Taborda Vlame Carlos (16th Century) National Museum of Ancient Art, Lisbon/Giraudon. p25 *Aurora Ascending the Heavens* by Julien de Parme (1736–99) Prado, Madrid.

p28 *Angel* by Sir Edward Burne-Jones (1833–98) Private Collection. p29 *The Dream of St Cecilia* by Paul Baudry (1828–86) Musee des Beaux-Arts, Moulins/Giraudon. p36 (top right) *Angel playing the Lute* by Giovanni Battista Rosso (1494–1540) Galleria Degli Affizi, Florence. p37 *Angels from the Side Walls in the Chapel* by Benozzo Gozzoli (c1420–97) Palazzo Medici-Riccardi, Florence. p40 *Angeli Laudantes* c1887 by Sir Edward Burne-Jones (1833–98) (designs for a window in Salisbury Cathedral, also for tapestries) Fitzwilliam Museum, University of Cambridge. p41 *Angel Playing a Trumpet*, detail from the Linaiuoli Triptych by Fra Angelico (c1387–1455) Museo di San Marco dell'Angelico, Florence. p44 *Angel* by Abbott Hanerson Thayer (1849–1921) National Museum of American Art, Smithsonian Inst. p45 *The Cloister or the World* by Arthur Hacker (1858–1919) Bradford Art Galleries & Museums. p48 *Angels at the Annunciation* by Fracesco Granacci (1477–1543) Galleria dell'Academia, Florence. p49 Detail of Heaven from *The Last Judgement* by Fra Angelico (c1387–1455) Museo di San Marco dell'Angelico, Florence. p52 *Angels Playing Musical Instruments* c1475–97 by Francesco Botticini (c1446–97) (attr) Museo della Collegiata di Sant' Andrea, Empoli. p53 *A Concert of Angels* by Spanish School (16th century) Museo de Bellas Artes, Bilbao/Index. p56 *The Story of Cupid and Psyche* by Jacopo del Sellaio (1441/2–93) Fitzwilliam Museum, University of Cambridge. p57 *An Angel holding a Glass Flask* by Juan de Valdes Leal (1622–90° Phillips, the International Fine Art Auctioneers. p60 *Angels*, detail from the *Madonna della Melagrana* by Sandro Botticelli (1444/5–1510) Galleia degli Uffizi, Florence. p61 (detail) *Aurora Ascending the Heavens* by Julien de Parme (1736–99) Prado, Madrid.
Back Jacket:
Slipcase (front) *Angel* by Abbott Handerson Thayer (1849–98) National Museum of American Art, Smithsonian Inst; (back)